KT-522-003

300 398 586 50

People who have helped the world

DESMOND TUTU

by David Winner

OTHER TITLES IN THE SERIES
Marie Curie by Beverley Birch (1-85015-092-3)
Father Damien by Pam Brown (1-85015-084-2)
Henry Dunant by Pam Brown (1-85015-106-7)
Mahatma Gandhi by Michael Nicholson (1-85015-091-5)
Bob Geldof by Charlotte Gray (1-85015-085-0)
Martin Luther King by Valerie Schloredt and Pam Brown
   (1-85015-086-9)
Florence Nightingale by Pam Brown (1-85015-117-2)
Albert Schweitzer by James Bentley (1-85015-114-8)
Sir Peter Scott by Julia Courtney (1-85015-108-3)
Mother Teresa by Charlotte Gray (1-85015-093-1)
Raoul Wallenberg by Michael Nicholson and
   David Winner (1-85015-109-1)
Coming Soon
Louis Braille by Beverley Birch (1-85015-139-3)
The Dalai Lama by Christopher Gibb (1-85015-141-5)
Louis Pasteur by Beverley Birch (1-85015-140-7)
Lech Walesa by Mary Craig (1-85015-107-5)

Picture Credits
Associated Press: 4; Omar Badsha: 46; BBC Hulton Picture Library: Mal Langsdon 45 (top left); Camera Press: Jacob Sutton 30; Fair Lady: 54 (both); International Defence and Aid Fund for Southern Africa: 8, 9 (both), 10, 12, 15 (both), 17, 22, 23, 26, 28, 35, 36 (top), 47 (below), 50-1, 52, 57; Link: Jillian Edelstein 42, 47 (top), Orde Eliason 29, 33, 38, 42 (top right and bottom left), 59 (top), Greg English 36, 40, 49; Peter Magubane: 34; Monitor: cover; Photo Source: C. Friend 7; Popperfoto: 16, 21; Reuters: Wendy Schwegmann 53; Reflex: Philip Littleton 59 (below); Rex Features: 37, Rogan Coles 44, Durand 11, 58 (top), Gunston 51 (above), J. Kuus 58 (below); Frank Spooner: J. Chiasson 51 (below), Chips Hire 45 (below right); Desmond Tutu: 19, 31; U.S.P.G.: Bryan Heseltine 6. Maps drawn by Geoffrey Pleasance.

To Caroline

Exley Publications would like to thank Desmond Tutu for allowing us to reproduce personal photographs in this book. We would also like to give special thanks to Mr John Allen, Mrs Crawford-Brown and other members of the Archbishop's Office for their advice and co-operation. We are most grateful to Shirley Du Boulay, author of *Tutu, Voice of the Voiceless* for generously sharing her research material, and to Wendy Coleman and Shirley Moulders who gave us great help with our research.

Published in Great Britain in 1989 by
Exley Publications Ltd
16 Chalk Hill, Watford, Herts WD1 4BN, United Kingdom.

Copyright © Exley Publications, 1989

British Library Cataloguing in Publication Data
Winner, David.
   Desmond Tutu.———(People who have helped the world).
   1. Tutu, Desmond.
   2. Church of England. *Province of South Africa—*
      Bishops—Biography—Juvenile literature.
   3. Bishops—South Africa—Biography—Juvenile literature.
   I. Title.   II. Series.
   283'.68'0924   BX5700.6.Z8.T/

ISBN 1-85015-087-7

All rights reserved. No part of this publication may be reproduced or transmitted in any form or by any means, electronic or mechanical, including photocopy, recording or any information storage and retrieval system without permission in writing from the Publisher.

Series conceived and edited by Helen Exley.
Picture research: Kate Duffy.
Research: Diana Briscoe.
Editorial: Margaret Montgomery.
Printed and bound in Hungary.

DESMOND TUTU

The brave and eloquent Archbishop struggling against apartheid in South Africa

David Winner

≣EXLEY

300398586

Protest in Cape Town

Even for the toughest campaigners against South Africa's cruel system of apartheid, the news of February 29, 1988 came as a shock.

After three years of savage repression, the whites-only government had finally banned the last remnants of legal opposition to their rule.

Over the years, the white government had crushed all black opposition. Now the non-racial United Democratic Front and sixteen other organizations were also silenced and their leaders arrested. It was clear that the South African government wouldn't let *anyone* oppose them, even when the protests were completely peaceful.

With all other black and anti-apartheid political leaders banned, in jail or in exile, the churches were now the only powerful organizations which could hope to challenge the government openly. Archbishop Desmond Tutu, the most respected, prominent and outspoken of all the church leaders, had now become one of the very few black leaders left who could lead the fight for justice. The new law, he said, was a "declaration of war".

He called on the great religious leaders of the country to gather in his cathedral in Cape Town to protest about it.

Archbishops, priests and ministers of almost every Christian organization came. First they all prayed together. Then, led by the tiny but courageous figure of Archbishop Tutu, they linked arms, marched out of the cathedral and headed off to the government headquarters a few hundred yards away, singing and praying as they went

They wished to hand in a petition. But their way was blocked by a line of heavily-armed riot police wearing pale blue shirts. As they reached the line, a policeman ordered the marchers to disperse.

Opposite:
Prayer and protest, 1988. Archbishop Desmond Tutu (middle) marches towards the police lines in Cape Town to protest about the banning of opposition groups. With him are all the main church leaders. On Tutu's left is Allan Boesak. On Tutu's right is Archbishop Stephen Naidoo. Within minutes, these brave people – now the strongest remaining voice of opposition to apartheid – would be arrested.

5

Land of cruel contrasts. Many of South Africa's twenty-one million black people are forced to live in crowded conditions like this, without electricity, running water or sewers. Racism is embedded in the country's laws which, at worst, directly cause poverty among Blacks. At best, they allow people to live in this kind of housing in a rich and beautiful land.

They refused. Instead, still singing, they knelt at the policemen's feet. For a moment, the police seemed not to know what to do. Then an order was given. Policemen's hands reached down roughly to drag Archbishop Tutu and the others away. They were under arrest. Soon after that, the police opened fire with water cannon on the rest of the crowd that had followed behind.

Tutu was one of the best-known church leaders in the world and the police dared not keep the religious men locked up for too long. His companions, including Allan Boesak, leader of the World Alliance of Reformed Churches, were almost equally famous. But, as far as the country's government was concerned, this peaceful protest amounted to troublemaking.

For more than forty years, the tyrannous white rulers of South Africa had tried to crush the black people by passing laws against them. Although

Blacks had lived in most parts of the country for centuries before white people had even arrived, they endured terrible hardships. While many Whites had servants and houses with swimming pools, most Blacks lived in desperate poverty without electricity, water or proper toilets. That resulted from the law.

Black fathers were forced to spend eleven months of the year away from their wives and children who often went hungry. That was allowed by the law.

Thousands of black people had to get up at three o'clock in the morning to get to work each day. Millions of workers had to travel long distances because black people weren't even allowed to live in the cities. That was the law.

Despite the fact that there were five times as many black people as white people, Blacks weren't allowed to vote. That was the law.

Black families who had lived in their homes for generations could be moved out and dumped in barren, desolated places hundreds of miles away on the word of a white government official. That was the law.

And anyone who protested about these or other injustices could be beaten or put in prison by the police or the army. That was also the law.

A few hours after the dramatic demonstration by the church leaders, a familiar question arose. If the law was the law, why didn't Archbishop Tutu believe it should be obeyed? With his eyes blazing, Tutu passionately gave his answer: "We are not talking about disobeying – we are obeying God!"

On the other side of the racial divide, many of South Africa's four-and-a-half million Whites live in surroundings like this in Stellenbosch. White homes have running water, electricity and rubbish collections.

The first Whites

The roots of the confrontation on the sunny streets of Cape Town that day went deep into history.

Discrimination by white people against black people in South Africa had been going on ever since white settlers arrived in the country nearly 350 years earlier – ironically in the Cape at almost exactly the spot where Archbishop Tutu had made his protest.

The first Europeans to come to live there were

Black servility at the hands of white rulers began hundreds of years ago. This picture shows black workers being supervised by white settlers in the early days of the Cape Colony in the seventeenth century.

the Dutch. In 1652, they set up a permanent settlement at the Cape, at the very tip of Africa. Ships of the powerful Dutch East India Company would stop there for fresh food, water and wood. The Dutch merchants and sailors enjoyed relaxing there in the near-perfect climate.

At that time, the huge land that is now called South Africa was inhabited by African people such as the Xhosa, Ndebele, Sotho, Tswana and Zulu. The unfortunate people who were closest to the new white settlers were two ancient, gentle, nomadic peoples: the San and the Khoikoi, whose way of life had been unchanged for thousands of years.

Tragically for them, the Cape soon became an important stopping place.

At first, the new arrivals from Europe got on well with the local people. But the peace did not last long. The settlers wanted local cattle and sheep for food. In the early days, they bought these animals. But later, as the Cape settlement grew, they stole them. The Khoikoi fought with spears, bows and arrows. But their resistance was doomed. The guns of the Whites were too powerful. Tens of thousands of Khoikoi were killed.

Tens more thousands died of infections brought by the settlers.

In the years that followed, boatloads of white settlers from Germany, France and the Netherlands gradually conquered the land all around. The Cape became a colony hundreds of miles in size. Most of these people were farmers and became known as "Boers". Over the years, the languages they spoke evolved into a new language called Afrikaans, and the Afrikaans-speaking Boers became quite prosperous.

But the Cape was now a place of great suffering for the Africans. The few surviving Khoikoi had to do menial jobs and were treated not much better than slaves. In addition, the Boers brought thousands of black slaves from other parts of Africa to the colony to work for them. Conditions were terribly cruel. Slaves or workers who tried to run away were killed or savagely punished.

This pattern of white conquest and black suffering was to be repeated tragically often in South Africa's bloody history.

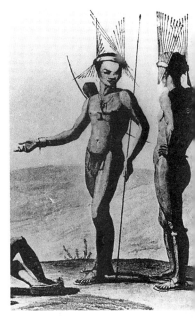

Above: The gentle San and Khoikhoi peoples, who suffered cruelly at the hands of the early settlers. Below: Boers drive the Xhosa people over the Fish River in the Wars of Dispossession in the 1780s.

The British take over

In 1815, after the wars against Napoleon, Britain took over the Cape Colony from the Dutch and became ruler of both the Boers and the Africans.

The British were as racist as the old rulers and it never occurred to them to think of black people as their equals. But at least in Britain the slave trade had been abolished and there was a move to abolish slavery throughout the British Empire. In 1834, the British rulers demanded that the Boers give freedom to their slaves.

The Boers, some of whom shot San people for sport, resented this. They disliked British rule and thought the British arrogant. As far as they were concerned, giving up their slaves would be a restriction on their *own* freedom!

The "Great Trek"

Boer protests against the anti-slavery laws had no effect. So, many of them decided to leave and set up their own countries, or republics, far away to

Boer settlers, called "voortrekkers", fight off attacking Zulus in the Battle of Vegkop during the "Great Trek". The Zulu armies fought bravely, but their spears and shields were no match for the Boers' deadly rifles. In this way, the Boers carved out their republics.

the north and east of the Cape. From 1835, six thousand Boers began to gather in groups and set off in wagons on their journey.

Today, Afrikaans-speakers (or Afrikaners) still think of this and other expeditions which followed as heroic exploits called the "Great Trek" and are proud of their ancestors, the "Voortrekkers", who made them.

The Voortrekkers may have thought they were heading off to an empty land. But they were really carrying out an invasion. In the years that followed, they clashed with African armies who were sent against them. The most powerful were the Zulus, who had themselves only recently conquered much of southern Africa. But even the much-feared Zulu spears and impis were no match for the modern Boer rifles and cannons, and in 1838 the Zulus were finally defeated.

Eventually, the Boers succeeded in carving out two new republics for themselves: the Orange Free State and Transvaal. Many black people there were put to work on land which had once been their own.

White Afrikaners are still proud of the Treks, which they mark each year on December 16 by dressing up in voortrekker clothes (like this woman) for ceremonies to remember their decisive defeat of the Zulus at the Battle of Blood River in 1838.

Gold and diamonds

Meanwhile, in the 1870s, the biggest reserve of diamonds ever to be found had been discovered at Kimberley.

As soon as Britain realized how much money was to be made out of this discovery, they decided to grab the diamond fields for themselves. In the next few years they swiftly conquered most of the remaining African kingdoms in the country and recruited thousands of black men to work in the new diamond mines in conditions little better than prisons.

At that time, of course, most Europeans did not see very much wrong with this way of doing things. In the name of "civilization", Europeans were still busily conquering countries all over the world to add to their empires, and no one was doing so more eagerly than the British. At best, conquered peoples could expect to be treated with disdain. At worst, they were treated with great cruelty. Unfortunately

Diamond mines at Kimberley in the 1870s. Discovery of the precious gems brought incredible wealth to the land. But the jewels brought only more suffering to most of the black people who worked in the mines. Note the cruelty of the overseer in the left hand part of the picture.

for everyone else, the age when Europeans thought all people should be treated as equals was still a very long way off.

Soon an even more momentous discovery was made in South Africa: vast gold fields were found in the Transvaal. Stretching three hundred miles, they formed the largest single concentration of gold in the world.

British people flocked there hoping to make their fortunes. But this soon led to a conflict with the Afrikaner republics. Who was to control the gold mines and the wealth? In 1899, this clash led to the Boer War between the Afrikaners and the British Empire.

It was a bitterly-fought war between the two

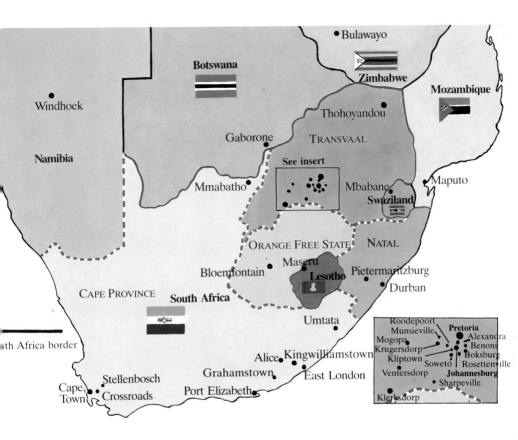

white peoples in the country and lasted for three years. The Boers suffered grievously. More than twenty thousand of their women and children died in British concentration camps. Eventually they were defeated.

Many thousands of Blacks, forced to fight on both sides, also died. But the history books hardly mention that.

South Africa and the surrounding countries, showing the important places in Desmond Tutu's life. In 1987, Tutu would become Archbishop of South Africa, as well as Lesotho, Namibia, Swaziland and Mozambique.

New hardship

South Africa had finally been united by force of arms and, with the passing of the South Africa Act in 1910, it was given a new name: The Union of South Africa.

Defeated Afrikaners and the victorious British now made peace with each other. In order not to upset the Afrikaners any further, the British gave them a large say in how the new country was run.

13

"You work for the white person in Johannesburg, in a huge house that probably has only two people in it. You have had to leave your home when it is still dark because transport is so inadequate. You go back home, you haven't seen your children and by the time you get home they have probably fallen asleep. Your home is probably no bigger than the living room of the house from which you have just come."

Desmond Tutu.

And that made life worse for South Africa's poor black people, whom the Whites insultingly called "kaffirs".

For decades, Blacks had been segregated from Whites in South Africa. But now many new laws discriminating against Blacks were passed by Afrikaner and English alike. Laws, like the Poll Tax, forced black people to work for Whites in order to earn money to pay the tax. Other laws controlled where black people should work and even where they could live.

Whites, who were a small minority, only about a fifth of the whole population, took most of the country for themselves, including all the best land. The few Blacks, Indians and so-called "Coloureds" who had been given the vote in the Cape had it taken away from them. A viciously racist law that made marriage between black and white people illegal was even passed!

Young Desmond

This was the world into which Desmond Mpilo Tutu was born on October 7, 1931 in Klerksdorp, a poor black township near the richest city in South Africa, Johannesburg.

Desmond Tutu's family was like that of millions of other black South Africans. Their home was small and crowded, there was no electricity or sanitation. Their water came from a communal tap in the dry, dusty street.

"... Or going to a shop with my father and hearing him addressed as 'boy'. I knew there wasn't a great deal I could do, but it just left me churned. I felt ... I felt ... poor man. What he must have been feeling, being humiliated in front of his son. Apartheid has always been the same systematic racial discrimination; it takes away your human dignity and rubs it in the dust and tramples it underfoot."

Desmond Tutu.

And the Tutus were subject to the same petty restrictions which affected all black people. Even though Desmond's father, Zachariah Tutu, was a proud and respected schoolteacher he had to carry a passbook like all other black people. White police would sometimes stop him on the street and demand his papers, which upset the young Desmond and struck him as being unjust.

But although the Tutu family was poor, it was usually happy and full of love. Their house was always packed with visitors. Desmond's mother, Aletha Tutu, worked as a domestic servant to a white family. She was so kind and gentle that she

Above: A typically desolate street scene in the dusty, black townships.
Left: A family without running water must make do with a tin bath in the open. This is the world into which Desmond Tutu was born: his bedroom was also the family dining room – and their sitting room. He describes himself as a "township urchin" who went barefoot to school.

was better known as "Komotso", which means "comforter of the afflicted". Desmond also got on well with his three sisters, one of whom died young.

Zachariah and Aletha couldn't afford to buy Desmond any toys, but he and his friends found other ways of having fun. They played football with old tennis balls, made model cars out of odds and ends. To make some money Desmond sometimes sold oranges or carried clubs as a caddy at a white golf club. Desmond Tutu later described himself as a barefoot "urchin".

A friend for life

Desmond was clever and worked hard at school, but he didn't yet show the saintly qualities for which he was later to become so famous! When he was about fourteen he and a friend, who used to share a fifteen mile train ride to Madibane High School in Sophiatown, became experts at cheating in card games they played with the other passengers. The workers actually enjoyed the fun: they nicknamed Desmond "the Professor" – and his exploits earned the boys a little extra pocket money.

Like other young Blacks, it always made Desmond feel very proud to hear stories about successful black people in other countries. He was thrilled by the music of famous black American musicians like Louis Armstrong and athletes like Jesse Owens who won four gold medals in the 1936 Olympics.

But there were kind and good white people as well. One day Desmond was out walking with his mother when they passed a tall, white priest. To Desmond's amazement, the priest did something that was unheard of for a white man in South Africa. He smiled warmly at Mrs. Tutu and politely raised his hat. The priest was a man who would later have a great influence on Desmond's life – Father Trevor Huddleston.

When he was fourteen, Desmond caught tuberculosis and became terribly ill. He lay in bed in a hospital full of dying men for nearly two years and, at one point, it looked as if he, too, might die.

But he also made a friend for life. Every day his

• *Father Trevor Huddleston (below right) is a brave and tireless campaigner against the evil of apartheid – and an inspiration to the young Desmond Tutu. Father Trevor, who became an archbishop and president of the Anti Apartheid Movement in Britain, is seen here in 1957. He and Desmond became lifelong friends.*

new friend, Father Trevor Huddleston, came to talk to him. It was a funny sight – tiny, skinny Desmond and the tall priest, who himself later became an archbishop, chatting away energetically to each other. Trevor Huddleston brought Desmond books to read and inspired him with a love of Christianity which never left him.

The Apartheid election

In 1948, disaster struck for all black South Africans. A general election was held in the country and the Whites, who were the only people allowed to vote, chose the openly racist Afrikaner Nationalist Party. It had campaigned with a new slogan, "apartheid", and promised to introduce extreme anti-black policies.

It was a fateful decision. At a time when the rest of the world was pulling back from the worst European excesses of the Colonial Age, the white people of South Africa were moving in completely the opposite direction.

As we have seen, racism, segregation and oppression of black people by Whites in South Africa had been going on for centuries. But now things became much worse. Racial prejudice and persecution of people because of the colour of their skin became a central part of the law of the land. The new government immediately set to work passing a flurry of evil new laws.

First came the Prohibition of Mixed Marriages Act and the Immorality Act which together made sex or marriage between Whites and "Non-whites" illegal. Then there was the Population Registration Act, under which every person in the country was arbitrarily classified as White, "Coloured" (the word created for people not regarded as White nor Black), Indian or "Native" (the word Whites used at the time for Blacks).

Classification under the Population Registration Act of 1950 was at first into three "racial" groups, but further laws made it even more complicated for those not considered white. "Coloureds" were subdivided into seven categories – Cape Coloured,

Schoolchildren demonstrate against the hated Group Areas Act during the 1950s. The law, which forced Blacks, Whites and so-called "coloured" people to live in separate parts of the country, was one of the main pillars of apartheid. The banner says in Afrikaans "We want to live with all races".

17

Apartheid is blatantly racist. This "whites only" holiday resort, at Meredale, thirty miles from Sharpeville refuses entry to black people. As apartheid became law in the years after 1948, similar signs banning black people from "Whites Only" beaches, park benches, buses and other amenities appeared throughout the country. Many such signs have been removed now, but the attitude they represent has not.

Cape Malay, Griqua, Indian, Chinese, Other Asiatic, Other Coloured. Africans were subdivided into eight groups according to language. But Whites, of course, remained as only one category despite any differences of origin e.g. English, Afrikaners, Portuguese, Greek, Japanese, Hungarians, Jewish, etc.

The word "race" originally meant "sharing a common ancestor". But in the nineteenth century biologists came up with a theory that human beings could be split up into different groups or "races". The study of genetics has now shown that the differences between people in any one population group are enormous compared with any differences there are between population groups. We can now confidently say that the idea of different "races" has no real meaning for humans. "Race" is only skin deep! Or, if you use the word with its original meaning, we all belong to only one race – the human race.

In South Africa you can see the nonsense that arises when you try to sort people into different "races". In the first ten years of the Act the Population Board tried some 45,000 cases. Behind these statistics lie broken families and untold heartache.

The Group Areas Act, which said each "race" had to live in a different place, and the Bantu Authorities Act were passed, setting up "dumping grounds" for groups whom Whites didn't want to have living near them. Separate schools, public transport, public toilets, even park benches were provided for the different groups. The police enforced the laws with increasing cruelty.

It was the beginning of a nightmare.

Leah

By 1950 Desmond had passed out of school with distinction. With the dreadful conditions under which black people lived, he was one of the tiny number who managed to get to university and, at first, wanted to become a doctor. But there was no money for him to study medicine, so he followed in his father's footsteps and became a teacher.

Meanwhile, he had met the woman he was to marry, Leah Shenxane. At first, the studious Desmond had been too busy reading even to notice her. But, later he fell in love and in 1955 Desmond and

"All Bantu persons in the white areas, whether they were born there or not, remain members of their respective nations. In other words, the fact that they work here does not make them members of the white nation – they remain Zulu, Tswana, Venda and so on. The basis on which the Bantu is present in the white area is to sell their labour here and for nothing else."

South Africa's Minister of Bantu Administration and Development.

"One government minister called those blacks who could no longer work 'superfluous appendages'. Our mothers and fathers, 'superfluous appendages'."
Desmond Tutu.

Desmond and Leah Tutu on their wedding day, July 2, 1955. Leah was a very powerful person in her own right. She would bring a sense of peace and happiness to Desmond in the years ahead.

"To say Tutu was a popular and successful teacher would be an understatement – he was a sensation. He was inspiring, even when teaching mathematics, a subject at which he had not himself excelled; he could keep order; he was loved; he fired his pupils with a new vision of life."

Shirley du Boulay, from "Tutu: voice of the voiceless".

Until the 1970s, black children and parents often had to build their own schools - like this one in the Eastern Transvaal. The walls were made of mud and the pattern in this picture was caused by the children's fingers as they plastered them.

There were only two school books in Miriam's class.

Leah got married. Soon they had their first of four children whom they named Trevor after Desmond's friend and teacher, Father Huddleston.

By this time Desmond had himself gained a B.A. degree and had become an exceptional and inspiring teacher at the Munsieville High School in Krugersdorp. Up to sixty students per class would listen spellbound to his lessons.

It looked as if he had found a true vocation. But it was not to last. In the mid-1950s, the government turned its attention to black schools and introduced the Bantu Education Act. It was one of the nastiest of all the new laws and the brainchild of the cleverest and most sinister apartheid leader, Dr Hendrik Verwoerd.

The purpose of this "education" law was actually to *stop* teaching black children anything they might want to learn. From now on, Blacks were to have a deliberately fifth-rate education.

Dr Hendrik Verwoerd wanted no more clever, well-educated, black people in South Africa. As far as he was concerned, the only job a black person was fit for was working for Whites.

"What is the point of teaching the Bantu child mathematics when it cannot use it in practice?" Verwoerd had asked. "If the Native in South Africa today is being taught to expect that he will live his adult life under a policy of equal rights, he is making a big mistake."

Desmond was horrified. He knew he could not go on being a teacher under this law. So he turned to the Church. His family was religious and he was already a passionately-committed Christian. He had been greatly influenced by people like Trevor Huddleston, so he decided to join a theological college and to become a priest.

Peaceful protest

From the very first days of apartheid, courageous peoples from all the cultural groups had protested against the system.

The first joint campaign of defiance was planned by the African National Congress (ANC) and the

South African Indian Congress (SAIC). It was led by a brilliant and brave young Johannesburg lawyer named Nelson Mandela.

Ever since the ANC was formed in 1912, protest against injustice had been peaceful. The new campaign was no different, though it was bigger and more dramatic than anything the country had ever seen before. The protests followed the principles of "non-violence" developed and first used in South Africa by Mahatma Gandhi forty years before. Later Gandhi put it into practice against British rule in India.

This method of peaceful protest became a model for Dr. Martin Luther King in the United States. And it would later be adopted by Desmond Tutu.

The aim of the Defiance Campaign was to make everyone realize how inhuman, unfair and stupid the apartheid laws were and to try to shame the government into changing the law by filling the prisons to overflowing.

Thousands of volunteers joined together to break laws like the ones which made it illegal for black people to walk in "White" cities at night. The protesters were careful always to tell the police in advance which laws they were going to break. And when they had broken them, they demanded to be arrested and put in prison! They also made sure that journalists were always on hand to see what happened.

The various congress movements, including the ANC, "Coloured" and White opponents of apartheid, now united to form the Congress Alliance. In 1955 the Congress Alliance published a "Freedom Charter" calling for an end to hunger, discrimination and injustice and demanding votes for all men and women and an equal share of the country's wealth.

Then, in 1956, the government arrested 156 Congress members of all backgrounds and colours, and put them on trial for treason. At the end of an incredibly long and famous trial, which lasted for five years, all the Congress members either had charges dropped or were found not guilty.

The trial brought apartheid to the attention of

A defence lawyer, Vernon Berrange, carried shoulder high at the end of the Treason Trial, which lasted from 1956 to 1961. The trial brought the situation in South Africa to the attention of the world – and the South African government suffered a humiliating reverse. All the defendants were found "not guilty". The courts and legal profession have battled to maintain justice in an increasingly brutal police state.

The Sharpeville Massacre which shocked the world. On March 21, 1960, sixty-nine unarmed men and women were shot dead by police during a peaceful demonstration against the hated Pass Laws. In South Africa, non-violent demonstration has repeatedly been met with violent repression.

the world, but it was soon overshadowed by the first of many bloody tragedies.

Massacre at Sharpeville

On March 21, 1960 five thousand peaceful demonstrators, protesting against the Pass Laws, gathered outside a police station in the township of Sharpeville. The crowd included many women and children.

Suddenly and without warning, the police opened fire. There were screams of terror and the crowd turned and fled in panic. But the police carried on shooting. Soon sixty-nine men and women lay dead in the dusty street and 180 others were wounded. But it was not to be the only time policemen would shoot dozens of unarmed black demonstrators in the back.

The Sharpeville massacre shocked the world and was followed by weeks of black protests and strikes. But it did not change apartheid for the better. The government, as it usually has done ever since, reacted to serious opposition with repression. The ANC and the other main black resistance movement, the Pan Africanist Congress (PAC), were outlawed. Many opponents of apartheid were put in prison without trial and quite often they were tortured. The police paid a huge network of Blacks to spy on other Blacks.

Blacks and a significant number of Whites who opposed apartheid were frustrated by the failure of their campaign of passive, non-violent resistance and were shocked by the killings at Sharpeville. For over fifty years, the ANC had used only peaceful means to make their protests. Now, in desperation, under the command of Nelson Mandela, the ANC set up a military wing that was called Umkhonto we Sizwe or "Spear of the Nation".

Mandela ordered that Umkhonto should never attack people, and should only sabotage places like electricity sub-stations. Some largely ineffective bomb attacks were carried out. The PAC's own military wing Poqo was more violent.

But by the end of 1964, both groups had been destroyed inside the country. The police captured all the leaders of Umkhonto at a house in a suburb of Johannesburg called Rivonia and put them on trial. Mandela, a man who had never killed and who had discouraged his followers from killing, was jailed for life. He is still seen by most Blacks as South Africa's rightful political leader.

Some ANC leaders, like Oliver Tambo, fled to keep the organization alive. But most of the other leaders were jailed along with Mandela.

Nelson Mandela, jailed leader of the African National Congress (ANC), has been in prison since 1962. Many Blacks still see him as their rightful leader and there has been a worldwide campaign for his release.

Tutu goes to London

Meanwhile, Desmond Tutu was deeply committed to his work in the Church. There were no signs of the outspoken political views which would one day make him famous. For three years he had studied theology and had now been ordained as a priest. He had been the star pupil at the seminary. So, in 1962, at the age of thirty-one, Desmond left South Africa for the first time to go to London to study

> *"His message was the love of God for all his children whatever and wherever they were. And it was God's love that shone from Desmond himself. We all felt – yes really felt – the love of God when Desmond was with us. The other commanding mark of his presence was joy. Whenever he came, to a Eucharist, to a meeting, to a party, to a meal – the whole company bubbled over with the sheer joy of being together with him. It was always as though the very place was lit up by his presence and permeated by his infectious laughter."*
>
> Charles Cartwright,
> Vicar at St Augustine's Church,
> Bromley, where Tutu was
> Honorary Curate.

theology at King's College and then to work as an assistant curate.

Far away from the growing misery in his own country, he fell in love with a new world. It took him and his wife, Leah, a while to get used to the freezing weather. But, compared to South Africa, London seemed to them like paradise.

Back home, every passing policeman was a potential enemy who might ask to see his passbook or make life unpleasant in other ways. By comparison, the British police seemed amazingly polite. Desmond and Leah could hardly believe it. Sometimes, they walked around central London late at night – just for the pleasure of *not* being arrested! They even stopped policemen to ask for directions, even when they knew where they were going.

One day Desmond was waiting to be served in a bank when a white man pushed in front of him to the head of the line. Desmond was astonished when the lady cashier politely told the man he would have to wait because Desmond was first. It would never have happened in South Africa in those days.

Happy days

He was also surprised at the freedom that British people had to express their opinions. He enjoyed going to Speakers' Corner in London's Hyde Park where policemen were on duty to *protect* speakers saying the most outrageous things, not to arrest them as they would have done at home.

At King's College, he was popular and quickly became a star student, getting first a degree in 1965 then, just a year later, a master's degree in theology. He also added Hebrew to the seven languages he already knew – Xhosa, Tswana, Venda, Zulu, English, Afrikaans and Greek!

He was also well-loved at the churches where he worked. His clowning, his powerful preaching, his loving kindness, his extrovert style (he used to tear around the parish on a motorcycle) broke down the usually formal British people. At the Tutus' huge farewell party there were many tears.

Tutu learned a great deal during his five years in England about religion, politics and kindness, which he gave and received in huge quantities. The experience also confirmed what he already knew – that black and white people could easily live together without conflict or bitterness.

But it was time for him to go home.

Police state

While Desmond was away, apartheid had mercilessly tightened its grip. Dr. Hendrik Verwoerd, the apartheid system's sinister high priest, had become Prime Minister in 1958.

At that time apartheid was still incomplete. Some areas of life were not affected by its laws. Blacks and Whites still even lived together in a few areas of the country and sometimes they played sports together.

Verwoerd was determined to change all that. He was a fanatical racist. Like many Afrikaners, he believed that Whites would be contaminated or corrupted by too close contact with black people. He was obsessed with people's colour and imagined the "white race" was in danger and needed to be protected if it was to survive.

In fact, the truth was the other way round. The people who needed protection were the black people – they urgently needed to be protected from apartheid and Dr. Verwoerd!

In 1960, the British prime minister, Harold Macmillan, made a famous speech in South Africa criticizing apartheid and saying that "a wind of change was blowing through Africa". But there wasn't much more practical help on offer from the outside. As before, the South African people had to face the apartheid storm mainly on their own.

After Sharpeville, Verwoerd unleashed a police assault on the remaining civil liberties in the country. Harsher apartheid laws meant strict segregation in every walk of life. Black people were banned from white buses, beaches, toilets and sports fields. If Blacks didn't have special permission to be out of their immediate area they would

"Desmond just won them over as he wins everybody over, not only by his example – he was obviously a very prayerful man – but also by his great sense of humour. He's always laughing, this most infectious laugh."

John Ewington, organist at the church of St. Mary the Virgin, Bletchingley, where Tutu was curate.

"They [the whites] laugh,
they love, they cuddle
babies, they weep, they eat,
they sleep – they are
human. But if they are
human, why, oh why can't
they see that we laugh too,
we love too, we weep too,
we cuddle babies too, we
eat, we sleep – why can't
they see that it is impossible
for things to go on like
this?"

Desmond Tutu, in an address
to the South African Institute
of Race Relations.

be arrested and put into prison.

But Verwoerd's new laws about the places where black people could live had the most far-reaching effects. He declared that because people of different "races" were "different", they should "develop separately". He, therefore, offered black people "independence" in their own lands, or "Bantustans". Most black people had never even seen their so-called "homelands". It was just an excuse to expel them from white areas and banish them to the poorest, most infertile areas of the country.

In 1913 and 1936, Whites had seized most of the country and all the best land for themselves, leaving only 13% specifically for the other groups who made up 80% of the population. But apartheid now made things even worse. The government used the law to give themselves power to kick Blacks out of their homes to make way for Whites. Blacks were now not citizens of South Africa – they were treated like migrant labourers.

Under the Group Areas Act whole black populations were "removed" from places where they had lived, sometimes for generations. Between 1960 and 1983, over three million people were dragged off or forced to leave their homes. If the people refused to move, the government simply sent police with trucks and bulldozers. They smashed down their homes and physically carried the people away, dumping them in barren, far-away places as if they were sacks of potatoes.

Sophiatown

One of the places where this had happened in the early days of apartheid was Sophiatown, a black community in Johannesburg. Nearly sixty thousand people lived there, many of them in houses they owned or had built themselves. Desmond Tutu knew Sophiatown well. He had lived there in Meyer Street when he was at school. His friend, Father Trevor Huddleston, was the priest there and, together with local people, he tried to save Sophiatown.

But they didn't stand a chance. One day two thousand policemen arrived with eighty trucks.

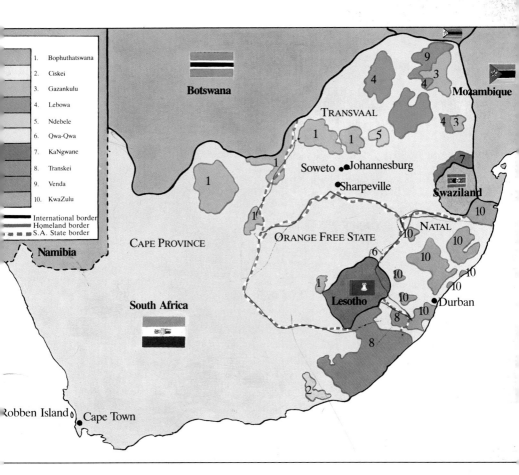

1.	Bophuthatswana
2.	Ciskei
3.	Gazankulu
4.	Lebowa
5.	Ndebele
6.	Qwa-Qwa
7.	KaNgwane
8.	Transkei
9.	Venda
10.	KwaZulu

International border
Homeland border
S.A. State border

Namibia

Botswana

Mozambique

TRANSVAAL

Soweto ••Johannesburg

Sharpeville

Swaziland

CAPE PROVINCE

ORANGE FREE STATE

NATAL

Lesotho

Durban

South Africa

Robben Island ◦ Cape Town

When all the Blacks had been taken away, their homes were destroyed. Sophiatown was razed to the ground and, in its place, the government built a new white suburb with a name which showed its contempt for its previous owners, "Triumph".

Broken families

Since the 1960s black people have been forced to live in remote, barren and dusty "homelands" or in ramshackle townships which are built just outside the rich white towns and cities.

This division, this *apartheid* (literally apart-ness) has caused untold, unbelievable misery to millions of people. It caused poverty and made it almost impossible for black people to succeed.

The ten "Homelands" are in fact a jigsaw of twenty seven large (and many more small) fragments of land, which were left for the Africans after the Whites had expanded to occupy the best areas. The "Homelands" consist of thirteen per cent of the country for eighty per cent of the people. The population densities are among the highest in Africa. There is little work available in these overcrowded and barren dumping grounds.

Perhaps the most tragic result was the breakdown of family life. Thousands and thousands of people were lost in the removals. With no telephones, no money, no home ownership, it was almost impossible to find anyone once they'd been moved.

If a person fell in love with someone from a different area it became illegal to visit. Married couples found themselves in different "homelands"!

Black fathers, with no land or job in the Bantustans, were desperately poor, and had to go to the cities to work. Mothers could only find jobs as live-in "nannies" or "girls" (domestic servants) to white families. No one without work was allowed to be in the cities. So the disabled, the old and the children were left behind. The meagre salaries of the parents were sent "home".

A mother struggles to do her household chores in the appalling conditions of the township of Zwelitemba. When families are forcibly removed, they are often abandoned on barren land in the country – it's the land no white farmers want.

Opposite: The forced removals policy uprooted three-and-a-half million black people from their homes and dumped them, often hundreds of miles away, in so-called "homelands" they had never seen. This family from Sophiatown was among the victims. Their home has been destroyed by government officials.

The Tutus return

Through these turbulent and sad years, Desmond Tutu worked his way up through the Church. He was an outstandingly brilliant scholar. On his return from Britain, with three degrees behind him,

Black people – Desmond Tutu included – are not allowed to sit down to eat in white areas. They are often served through hatches, like this one, at the side or back of the building.

he became a lecturer in Greek and theology at Alice, in the Cape Province.

He continued his deeply religious life of long hours of meditation and days of fasting and silence. His worship, his Christianity, were deep commitments. There were no outward signs that he would one day become the most famous political figure in South Africa.

Tutu was not politically naive. The blazing injustice of the South African laws struck home to him every day.

No matter how many degrees he earned, no matter how senior he became, no matter how honest or good he was, he still could not even sit at a table to eat in a dirty "white" café. He had to go round the side to be served from a hatch for "non-whites".

He could not send his kids to a white school, nor own a home in a white area. He could not vote.

Yet, Tutu put religion first. And, as the years passed and the demands on his time grew, this never changed.

Turning point

A dreadful incident in 1968 was one of the turning points for Desmond.

While he was lecturing at Alice, he also worked as the chaplain at Fort Hare University, one of only three universities for black students in South Africa. It was the year student revolution broke out all over the western world and the students at Fort Hare staged their own less aggressive strikes and protests, asking for very moderate improvements.

At one point, five hundred students, out of a total of 550, were holding a peaceful sit-down on the university lawns. It was a very mild protest compared with the riots and massed marches that had taken place in France, West Germany and the USA.

During the morning the students were warned that they should abandon the protest by two that afternoon – or face expulsion. They sat on, quietly talking and reading.

At 2 o'clock the police arrived and reacted with terrifying brutality. At gunpoint, the students were

"If they [white people] can tell themselves that an eighteen-year-old white child has more wisdom and more capacity to make decisions than I do, it must mean that they believe a black person – no matter how high he may go, no matter how educated he may be – is still less than that child, because an eighteen-year-old white can vote and I can't."

Desmond Tutu.

The happy Tutu family. Desmond, Leah and their four children in London in 1964 while Desmond studied for his degree. The children are (from the left) Trevor, Theresa, Naomi and Mpho.

31

made to collect their belongings and leave.

In a land where university education meant long years of sacrifice for all black students, this was a draconian punishment. It made it virtually impossible for the victims to go to university ever again. It certainly broke many lives.

Desmond was deeply shocked. At that time, he was quite unpolitical in his views, but he threw himself into the thick of the trouble by standing up for the students.

He was shaken to the core by the police violence. Nearly twenty years later he remembered: "I never cried quite as much as I did then.

Dean of Johannesburg

After three years as lecturer in Alice, Tutu moved to the small country of Lesotho where he taught at the National University. By the early 1970s he was well-known within the Church in southern Africa. He was a respected scholar and determined to rise rapidly within the Church hierarchy.

Between 1972 and 1975 Tutu went back to London to work as associate director of the Theological Education Fund. During these years, he visited many countries to allocate funds. He saw many of the world's trouble spots and gained wide experience which would be invaluable to him in the vital years ahead.

His reputation was growing with every passing year and his kindness, wisdom and courage became widely known. He also increasingly began to speak out against the injustice that was all around him.

In 1975, aged 44, Tutu was catapulted to prominence when he was elected the Dean of Johannesburg. No black man had ever been appointed to such a senior position in the Anglican church before. From now on, any speech he uttered would be quoted. It was a very public position indeed.

Black people were excited, delighted and proud of him. They were even more pleased with one of Desmond's first decisions. He showed his support for ordinary black people by refusing to move into the plush home in a white suburb where previous deans had lived. Instead, he and his family would

"The school must equip him [the African] to meet the demands which the economic life of South Africa will impose upon him…. There is no place for the native in European society above the level of certain forms of labour…. Race relations cannot improve if the wrong sort of education is given to the Africans; if the result of education is the creation of frustrated people; when it creates people who are trained for professions not open to them."

Dr. Verwoerd,
Minister of Education.

live ten miles away in Soweto, the giant, sprawling slum-ridden black township where most of the Blacks who worked in Johannesburg lived.

But Desmond, bubbling with life and energy, never let himself be depressed by his surroundings. Some white members of his new church, St Mary's, were taken aback by the warmth of his style of worship. They weren't used to being asked to hug and kiss each other!

Letter to the Prime Minister

It was now that Tutu took his first highly controversial public political step. It would rocket him to fame in South Africa. Tutu, aware of the tensions building up in the townships, especially among young people, wrote a very polite and respectful open letter "from one Christian to another" to the new Prime Minister, John Vorster. In it he appealed for justice and an end to racial oppression in South Africa. "I write to you, Sir, because, like you, I am deeply committed to real reconciliation with justice for all, and to peaceful change to a more just and open South African society in which the wonderful wealth and riches of our country will be shared more equitably ..."

He prophesied that without justice and freedom for black people, all South Africans, both Black and White, faced a terrible and bloody future.

"I have a growing, nightmarish fear that unless something drastic is done very soon then bloodshed and violence are going to happen in South Africa almost inevitably.

"Black people," he said, could "take only so much and no more.... A people made desperate by despair, injustice and oppression will use desperate means. I am frightened, dreadfully frightened, that we may soon reach a point of no return, when events will generate a momentum of their own, when nothing will stop their reaching a bloody denouement which is 'too ghastly for words'."

He pleaded with the Prime Minister to scrap the hated Pass Laws and let black people live in the "white" cities and he urged him to talk to black leaders to find an end to the nightmare.

Apartheid deprives Blacks of rights that other people take for granted. This farm worker and his wife were sacked for arguing with another worker. Now they walk for many miles carrying their few possessions with them. Many farm workers have lived on their farms for generations. If the white owner sacks a worker, the worker and his family immediately become homeless and illegal. If they can't find work, their only solution is to go to a "homeland" – a homeland they have never seen.

Soweto, June 16, 1976. Schoolchildren singing and dancing in peaceful protest about a new law that says their lessons must be taught in Afrikaans.

Vorster virtually ignored the letter. He refused to answer Desmond's arguments and wrote back accusing him of trying to "make propaganda".

But the terrible events which Desmond predicted were to come even sooner than anyone had thought possible.

The children of Soweto

For several years, a new political movement had been growing among young Blacks. This was Black Consciousness, which encouraged them to be proud of their history and culture and not to consider themselves inferior to Whites. They were politically alert and all too aware of the humiliations suffered by their parents' generation. They were not going to be so long-suffering.

Then in 1976, just two months after Tutu's prophetic letter, the spark was lit. The government made an amazingly tactless move. It ordered that, from now on, school lessons should not be taught

The same demonstration less than an hour later. The police have opened fire and twelve-year-old Hector Petersen is dead – the first of nearly six hundred youngsters to be killed in what became an uprising that shook South Africa for months.

in English, but in Afrikaans – the hated language of the oppressors.

At first the student protests were quiet and peaceful – as usual, they were ignored by the government. Then, on the fateful day of June 16, 1976, black schoolchildren gathered in the smoky, dusty streets of Soweto and marched from school to school, their numbers growing. Finally, a singing, laughing, excited crowd of fifteen thousand children waving placards converged on the Junior Secondary School in Orlando.

The reaction of the police was more terrible than anything since the massacre at Sharpeville.

They opened fire on the children. A twelve-year-old boy named Hector Petersen was the first of

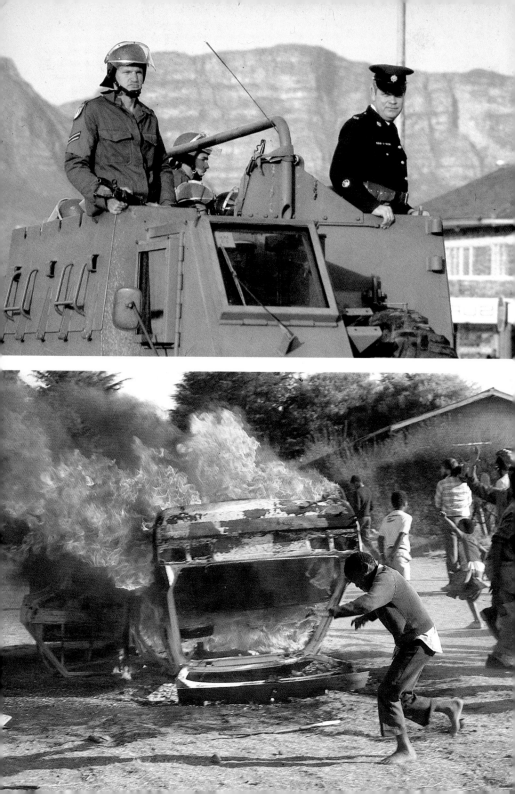

After 1976, young Blacks moved into the frontline of the struggle against apartheid. The servility of their parents had gone forever as the young people, like this girl, walked tall – proud to be black.

many to be killed. Over the next few weeks, hundreds of other youngsters all over the country died as young Blacks rioted in sympathy and defiance.

Incredibly, the demonstrations in Soweto quickly turned into a national black uprising against apartheid, led by the schoolchildren. There had never been anything like it.

After several months, and many hundreds of deaths and thousands of injuries, the uprising eventually came to an end. It failed to bring an end to apartheid. But it had shaken the system to its foundations. People all over the world were outraged by the savagery of the police and soldiers. Repeated scenes of police opening fire with automatic rifles on small groups of unarmed, singing students had an electrifying effect on the world. Attention was once again focussed on South Africa.

Desmond Tutu was unable to be with his people

Opposite: Black riots against apartheid swept South Africa for months after the killings at Soweto.
Top: White policemen roamed the turbulent townships in armoured cars trying to put down the uprising while young Blacks vented their anger on the streets (bottom).

Inches away – but worlds apart. White schoolboys leaving a cadet camp in Vereeniging pass a group of black youngsters their own age from a township. Because of the apartheid laws, these white boys will never see the homes of the black majority in their own land. Unfortunately, the black boys will see inside white homes at the very least as servants. Most of them will work in white-owned businesses.

through this tragic period. In 1976, after only two years as Dean of Johannesburg, he was appointed Bishop of Lesotho, the small, independent country surrounded by South Africa.

It was frustrating – heartbreaking – to be away from his people during these troubled days, but Desmond Tutu committed himself fully to his work as Bishop. It was another vital part of his training for his future world role.

When Steve Biko, the founder and leader of the Black Consciousness Movement, was murdered by the South African police, Desmond was called back to speak at his funeral. It was an event full of anguish. Biko was a wise and gifted man. He was only thirty years old, but he had looked set to become the greatest Black leader since Nelson Mandela.

Biko's death, from beatings and torture while he was being held in police custody, had been a shattering blow which shocked all freedom-loving South Africans and the rest of the world. Desmond's words expressed these feelings: "We are numb with grief, and groan with anguish 'Oh God, where are you? Oh God, do you really care – how can you let this happen to us?'" Desmond had not met Steve Biko, but he shared his dream of making Africans proud, equal and able to achieve a real peace and equality with Whites.

Pray for white people too

Desmond also passionately believed that apartheid damages Whites as well as black people because it makes them lose their humanity. The Justice Minister, Jimmy Kruger, had shown just how shockingly true this was when he said that Biko's death "leaves me cold". Of all human beings, Kruger was "the most to be pitied," said Desmond. "What has happened to him as a human being when the death of a fellow human being can leave him cold?"

So he asked the mourners to pray for the white people of South Africa; for the rulers, the police, especially the security police who had murdered Steve Biko, so that they too "may realize they are human beings."

Tutu's words were not popular with everyone at the funeral because people were very angry about what had happened to Steve Biko. But Tutu made them look at the way that white people in South Africa are also victims of apartheid.

It may seem hard to believe, but many Whites have no clear idea about what life is like for Blacks. For instance, white children who have black nannies to love and look after them and have dozens of expensive toys to play with, simply cannot imagine what life is like for black children in the same country. They don't see how black people live because white people are not allowed to go into the townships or so-called "homelands". In the same way that two thousand years ago Romans thought that owning slaves was perfectly normal, white South Africans are also brought up to think that separating people because of their "race" is a sensible, good thing.

What makes things worse is that South African radio and television stations are so heavily-censored

"You are brainwashed into an acquiescence in your oppression and exploitation. You come to believe what others have determined about you, filling you with self-disgust, self-contempt and self-hatred, accepting a negative self-image ... and you need a lot of grace to have that demon of self-hatred exorcised, when you accept that only white races really matter and you allow the white person to set your standards and provide your role models."

Desmond Tutu.

"You would have thought by this time they [the black people] would be saying 'To hell with all white people'. They say 'Ah-ah, we don't hate white people, we hate apartheid, we hate injustice, we hate oppression and we are for goodness, for justice and for peace.... We are going to stride into this great future, this new South Africa, this non-racial South Africa where people will count not because of the colour of their skins, but where people count because they have been made in the image of God.'"

Desmond Tutu.

"Apartheid comprehensively contradicts the Bible and Christian teaching. That is why it is totally evil and totally immoral." Bishop Desmond Tutu is a passionate preacher.

by the government that they give a very peculiar impression of the world. People in other countries know more about the injustice in South Africa than South Africans themselves. As in many closed political systems, much money is put into propaganda. Every protest or act of hooliganism in Europe is shown on South African television. But the South African riots do not appear. Every problem in the rest of Africa is highlighted, but similar problems in South Africa are just not shown.

One of the most tragic effects of years of propaganda was that it had worked on *all* people. Black people also thought of themselves as inferior: they saw few successful black leaders to imitate. People such as Steve Biko and Tutu helped to counter this. There was now a growing confidence and pride. Asians and "Coloureds" now wanted to be called "Black". It was necessary to stop the deliberate government strategy of "divide and rule".

One example of this slanted news reporting is

the unfair and distorted way Desmond Tutu is shown on television in his own country. His wit, love and lack of bitterness shine through when he preaches or gives interviews. But South African television usually edits his appearances to give viewers the idea that he must be a slightly crazy, bitter revolutionary. If he gives an hour-long talk on preventing a bloodbath, he will be shown waving his arms vigorously (as he regularly does!) while the commentator talks. Then Tutu's voice will sound for just one phrase: "... there is going to be a blood-bath."

He is regularly misquoted by newspapers.

Nothing could be more unfair. All his life, Desmond Tutu has believed in and preached for love, peace and reconciliation. He believes that apartheid is a completely evil system. He says that because God created all people equal, laws which allow one group to discriminate against others are blasphemous crimes against God.

He has often shown anger over injustice – but never hatred for white people. Like most black people, he simply yearns for the day when apartheid is gone and all South Africans can live together happily as equals at peace without resentment or violence on either side.

The tragedy is that most South Africans never hear what he is actually trying to say to them.

Into the hot seat

In 1978, after just two years as Bishop of Lesotho, Tutu was given a very senior, and highly controversial, job which he again felt compelled to take. He returned from Lesotho to South Africa – this time for good.

The new job was to last seven years and would be his most demanding and politically sensitive yet. He was appointed the general secretary of the South African Council of Churches (SACC). He remained a bishop, but without a diocese. He was still the black man with the highest position in the South African Anglican church. It was a time when the whole of South Africa was again on the boil and

"The Bishop scares the government because it feels threatened by his articulateness and self confidence ... he is more than just the ultimate 'cheeky kaffir' – he represents a threat to their basic concepts about race upon which they have built their whole life and ideology."
Dr. Beyers Naude, an Afrikaner churchman.

"What do they think they accomplish when they attack me personally? Do they think that by tarnishing my character they are changing the facts of the evil system I am denouncing?"
Desmond Tutu.

41

the country's churches were becoming increasingly outspoken in their attacks on apartheid.

After Soweto and the death of Steve Biko, the South African government knew it had to make some changes. Over the next few years the black middle class continued to grow rapidly. Businesses needed all the talented people they could get. Despite the government, the people were ignoring many laws. It looked as though the country could grow out of apartheid.

Hopeful signs

Some of the most obvious symbols of apartheid were indeed abolished. For instance, the laws forbidding Blacks to go to "Whites-only" public parks and toilets were scrapped. Black and white athletes played sports together in a way that would have been impossible a few years earlier. Blacks were now allowed to set foot inside "international hotels" in the cities. The new prime minister, P.W. Botha, even told the Whites: "Apartheid is a recipe for permanent conflict ... we must adapt otherwise we shall die."

But these were to prove to be hollow words. The government seemed to have no real intention of getting rid of the fundamental basis of apartheid. Great reforms were promised and slick Afrikaner politicians, aware of South Africa's terrible reputation, now tried to persuade the world that apartheid was becoming a thing of the past.

But the hated Pass Laws and Group Areas Act remained intact. The system was still cruel. Many thousands of people were still being evicted from their homes. Blacks were still denied even basic political rights.

In any case, the improvements which did take place would hardly be enough to satisfy an angry new generation of young Blacks. After Soweto, young Blacks were feeling brave, determined and impatient for change. They would never again accept apartheid as their parents had done.

From now on, the government would only be able to keep control by resorting to ever more brutal methods.

"Let me make this point categorically. The situation in South Africa is violent. And the primary violence is the violence of apartheid. It is the violence of forced population removals. It is the violence of detention without trial and of mysterious deaths in detention. It is the violence that forces children to be stunted through a deliberately inferior education system, or of the migratory labour system which systematically destroys black family life."
Desmond Tutu.

Opposite: A vision of the future? This happy multiracial class is becoming increasingly common in South Africa. It offers a glimpse of how the country might be after apartheid and bears out Desmond Tutu's vision of racial harmony.

43

"Why should they be afraid of me? I don't even have a vote in my country.

Why should they be frightened of one little black man who goes about saying a few things, if what he is saying is untrue?"

Desmond Tutu.

Desmond Tutu became one of the most eloquent voices against apartheid during the late 1970s and early 1980s. But he always spoke against violence and hatred and for reconciliation and brotherhood between Whites and Blacks. Here he is addressing a crowd at the funeral of fourteen victims of violence in the black township of Kwathema in 1985.

"An insect in dark glasses"

Against this background Desmond Tutu was becoming a world figure and one of the best-known of all the voices of South African protest.

He had always been first and foremost a churchman rather than a politician. But in his new job he showed he could also be a fearless and tireless campaigner. In almost every speech, article, sermon and interview in South Africa and abroad he denounced apartheid and called for justice. He demanded an end to tyranny. "Apartheid comprehensively contradicts the Bible and Christian teaching," he stormed. "That is why it is totally evil and totally immoral."

But, Tutu never preached violence. Instead, his message, repeated over and over again with his unequalled passion as an orator, was one of peace and reconciliation.

Nevertheless, many white people wished he would "keep politics out of religion". They weren't used to having a black bishop telling them they were in the wrong. Desmond became the target of increasingly cruel and unfair attacks from the government and the press who tried to portray him as a violent and dangerous revolutionary. Many of these attacks were spiteful as well as ridiculous. One newspaper cruelly referred to him as "an insect in dark glasses".

But there was a more sinister side to this hatred: he began to receive death threats and abusive phone calls. Whenever this happened, Desmond startled the caller by carefully listening until the threat was over, then saying a prayer for the caller before hanging up.

Because of his outspoken opposition to apartheid, many white people seemed to think he was the devil incarnate and Tutu later joked "I really do have horns underneath my funny bishop's hat." But behind all the laughter and clowning, Tutu was an extremely sensitive man. He told friends that he loved to love and to be loved: the jibes, insults and threats always hurt him deeply.

Whatever South Africans thought of him, people in the rest of the world had started to listen to

Four faces of Bishop Tutu. Top left: At prayer during a visit to America in 1984. Bottom left: Giving an interview to journalists. Above: At home in Johannesburg in 1985.

Tutu enjoys his own Christmas party, 1987. Archbishop Tutu has turned his home in Cape Town into a community centre, where black and white children could play together.

Omar Badsha, the photographer who took this picture, was imprisoned without trial in 1988.

Desmond Tutu. The fact that he was a natural-born TV performer certainly helped! His warmth, honesty and intelligence, a famous deep chuckle and sense of fun meant that almost everyone who met him liked and respected him immediately. Wherever he went, journalists thronged to talk to him.

Sanctions call

But his role as leader of the South African Council of Churches, the SACC, increasingly led Tutu into clashes with the government who started to harrass and snipe at him.

In 1979, his passport was taken away because, in a television interview in Denmark, he had asked the Danes to stop buying South African coal as a protest against apartheid. Britain's Archbishop of Canterbury and dozens of other bishops came to Desmond's defence and the government was eventually forced to give him back his passport.

In 1980 Bishop Tutu was arrested on a protest march and was treated like a criminal: the police photographed him, took his finger prints and fined him. On a visit to Europe in 1981, he called apartheid "the most evil regime since the Nazis" and discussed the problems in South Africa with the Pope at St Peter's in Rome.

As soon as Desmond returned to South Africa, the government took away his passport again, this time for more than a year.

From now on, whenever he went to another country, he begged the world – particularly Britain, the USA and West Germany – to stop trading with South Africa. Tough economic sanctions, he said, were the last way of putting peaceful pressure on the South African government to give up apartheid "before it is too late".

With extreme reluctance, Britain, the USA and West Germany eventually agreed to impose minor sanctions, but not enough to really hurt the South African economy.

Tutu's calls for sanctions have caused more anger in South Africa than anything else he ever did. People saw him as a "traitor". But he always defended his statements by saying that there is no other non-violent way to protest. All the other black leaders have been banned or jailed – including the non-violent ones.

The government now tried to destroy the credibility of the SACC and set up a commission to investigate its activities. But Desmond defended stoutly and, after a protracted legal enquiry, proved the SACC had behaved impeccably.

In one way, all this unwelcome attention could be taken as a compliment. The government attacked Desmond because they understood how popular, respected and, therefore, dangerous to them he was becoming.

Peace prize winner

But a very much greater award awaited him.

On October 15, 1984, Desmond Tutu was chosen to receive the Nobel Peace Prize, arguably the world's most respected and prestigious award. The award was meant as a gesture of support not only for Desmond and the SACC but for "all individuals

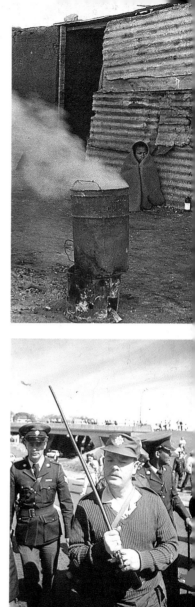

Desmond Tutu describes apartheid as "the most evil regime since the Nazis". A black child huddles outside a "resettlement shack" (above) while police, like these men carrying whips know as sjamboks, supervise the system.

"This award [the Nobel Peace Prize] is for you – Mothers, who sit near railway stations trying to eke out an existence, selling potatoes, selling mealies, selling pigs' trotters.
This award is for you – Fathers, sitting in a single-sex hostel, separated from your children for eleven months of the year.
This award is for you – Mothers in squatter camps, whose shelters are destroyed callously every day and who have to sit on soaking mattresses in the winter rain, holding whimpering babies and whose crime in this country is that you want to be with your husbands.
This award is for you – three and a half million of our people who have been uprooted and dumped as if they were rubbish. The world says we recognise you, we recognise that you are people who love peace."
Desmond Tutu, on being awarded the 1984 Nobel Peace Prize.

and groups in South Africa who, with their concern for human dignity, fraternity and democracy, incite the admiration of the world."

That's how it was taken inside the country. South Africa's black people and anti-apartheid campaigners went wild in celebration. At the SACC's offices, the staff hugged each other, laughed and sang for hours. "Hey, we are winning!" said Desmond delightedly when he heard the news.

The prize was a fantastic boost for the anti-apartheid struggle and congratulations flooded in from all over the world: from the President of the USA, Ronald Reagan, to the Pope, from Britain's Terry Waite and the Polish former Solidarity leader Lech Walesa, who had himself won the prize a few years earlier, to the Prime Minister of India, Mrs. Indira Gandhi.

To Desmond's great regret and sadness, the South African government in Pretoria didn't say a word about the award, let alone congratulate the prize winner. The country's leaders seemed almost stunned into silence.

Bomb scare

Before the award ceremony in Oslo, the capital of Norway, there came more wonderful news: Desmond Tutu had been elected Bishop of Johannesburg. Then came the presentation of the Nobel Peace Prize. It was a joyous and spectacular occasion – and more eventful than anyone would have wished. During four days of celebrations, thousands of students staged a beautiful and moving torchlight procession and there was a grand festival of folk music with the churches.

But half way through the grand prize-giving banquet, there was a warning that someone had planted a bomb. Desmond, his wife, Leah, the King of Norway and all the guests had to leave their seats while police searched the building. Outside, refusing to let the interruption get in the way of a great occasion, they sang "We Shall Overcome" (led, of course, by Desmond!) and, after an hour's wait, the police declared the hall safe and let everyone back inside. A choir from South Africa sang the beautiful black anthem "Nkosi Sikele' iAfrika" and Desmond finally got his prize.

In his acceptance speech, he typically called for peace and justice in South Africa and echoed the words of the Old Testament prophet Micah with the words: "Let us beat our swords into ploughshares".

Bishop Demond Tutu was now unquestionably a major figure in world affairs. He could talk on equal terms with the most powerful leaders. And the media flocked to hear him as never before. Tutu's message was beamed across the world. In America and Europe, millions of people who had never thought about apartheid before now heard about it through him.

There were other advantages too. Being a Nobel Laureate also gave him some much-needed protection, status and influence at home.

He was going to need it.

Black anger erupts

In 1984 black anger, which had been bubbling under the surface of repression, erupted more explosively than ever before.

Perhaps surprisingly, the trigger for the volcanic new wave of unrest was a suggested reform. In 1983, Prime Minister Botha had put forward a plan to give so-called "Coloureds" and Indians a vote for the first time for decades – though only for their own separate parliaments.

It was not a very tempting offer – the white people would still be keeping all the real power for themselves.

For Blacks the plan was worse than an insult. Although they were the vast majority of the population, they were totally ignored. The government claimed that black people were not even citizens of South Africa! This was because, in the 1970s, the government had said they were citizens of the Bantustans, the so-called "independent" black "homelands", scattered throughout the poorer areas of the country.

"Tutu is a hero figure in the black townships, especially since he won the Nobel Prize and demonstrated to a population haunted by its second-class status that one of them could become a world figure."
Allister Sparks, from "The Observer", August 4, 1985.

1985: The new face of protest. These schoolchildren are part of a crowd of three thousand marching on government offices to vent their feelings after black homes in Tsakane were destroyed by government officials in 1985.

As South Africa burned in 1984 and 1985, mass funerals, like this one, became a focus for political protest. Here members of the multiracial United Democratic Front (UDF) mourn their dead.

This was a farcical idea – most black people had never even visited the "homelands" they were supposed to belong to and no other country in the world recognized them.

Black resentment could no longer be contained. Demonstrations broke out everywhere and the protests lasted for months. As before, the police and army reacted with violence.

In March 1985, on the twenty-fifth anniversary of the Sharpeville Massacre there was another massacre. Twenty unarmed demonstrators were shot dead by police at Uitenhage, in the extreme south of the country. South Africa was engulfed in

a seemingly endless wave of protest, riots and strikes, which were all met by arrests, detentions and the police and army's use of shotguns, tear gas or rhino-hide whips called sjamboks. Police roamed the townships in their Hippo and Casspir riot vehicles, adding to the atmosphere of terror. No one was safe. Not even the young. Thousands of children were locked up without trial.

But there was a terrifying new element. Radical young Blacks in the townships calling themselves "comrades" were now venting their fury and frustration on those, often older Blacks, they accused of "collaborating" with apartheid.

Above: Another township, another blazing car. The police and army could not break the spirit of black resistance. Then in 1988 came the most brutal and repressive laws South Africa had ever seen. Even reporting violence could mean imprisonment without trial.

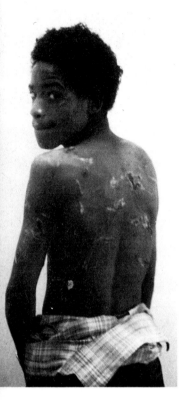

Thirty thousand people were arrested – many without charge – including thousands of children, some as young as eleven years old. Some were tortured. Others have not been released and the police have refused to tell families where their children are held.

"What country detains 11-year-olds because they are a threat to the security of the state?"

Desmond Tutu.

A cruel new method of killing came to symbolize this anger – the dreaded "necklace", a petrol-filled car tyre that was put over victims' heads and set alight. Dozens of people were murdered in this horrible way. Black community leaders, policemen and informers feared for their lives. Almost every time there was a demonstration, someone got killed on one side or the other.

Desmond, who was everywhere in the thick of things making speeches, conducting huge funerals that became political rallies, was appalled. His dream of a peaceful end to apartheid, or, as he now put it "a *reasonably* peaceful" end to apartheid, seemed a long way off.

"I will pack my bags"

One day in July, 1985, Desmond came to the unhappy township of Duduza in the Transvaal for the funeral of four men killed by police.

In the months of protest, Duduza had become a sullen, angry battleground and was now scarred. In one week, the police had killed ten black people and they had also set fire to the homes of the activists. In retaliation, most of the homes of black policemen and local leaders had been burned by angry crowds.

Now Desmond Tutu begged the mourners to turn away from violence and to try to change apartheid by peaceful means. But the crowd ignored his words. Suddenly they spotted a black man they thought was a police spy and surged forward to kill him, overturning and setting fire to his car and shouting, "let the dog die!"

Desmond pleaded with them to no avail. Killing was wrong whatever the provocation, he said. They would not listen to him. He had to act. While two other bishops created a diversion, Desmond put his life on the line and flung himself into the seething crowd, dragging the terrified and bleeding man away to safety.

But a few days later, after Tutu had left, there was another funeral in Duduza. The crowd thought that a young mother named Maki Shosana also

worked for the police. A screaming mob turned on her and beat and burned her to death in full view of the television cameras. Horrifying pictures of the killing were seen across the world.

Tutu was shocked. In a packed sports stadium in KwaThema, where he was conducting yet another funeral, he spoke his mind.

"If you do that kind of thing again, I will find it difficult to speak for the cause of liberation," he stormed. "If the violence continues, I will pack my bags, collect my family and leave this country I love so passionately. Our cause is just and noble. That is why it will prevail and bring victory to us. You cannot use methods to attain the goal of liberation that our enemy will use against us."

Such views made him unpopular with impatient, radical Blacks who were also angry that Tutu agreed to meet the Prime Minister, P.W. Botha, in the middle of the crisis. But Tutu insisted that true

Bishop Tutu holds an all-night vigil with the people of the small village of Mogopa. They had lived there for generations, but the next day their homes, church and school were bulldozed and the people were forcibly taken away. White farmers bought their cattle at a quarter of its value.

After his enthronement as the first black Anglican Archbishop of Cape Town, Desmond and Leah Tutu moved out of Soweto into the luxurious Archbishop's house in Cape Town. Leah did not want to leave her work in Johannesburg where she led an organization that championed the rights of domestic servants. But, as she had always done, she stood by Desmond as they moved into probably the most difficult and dangerous chapter of their lives.

54

peace could only come through dialogue – and even the leader of such an inhuman government was a human being. In any case, Tutu was even more unpopular with the government.

Meanwhile President Botha had declared a "state of emergency" giving the police and army savage new powers of repression and imposing severe restrictions on the media. South Africa was more of a police state than ever before.

Archbishop Tutu

Then in 1986 came the news that Desmond Tutu had been elected the new Archbishop of Cape Town – the highest position in South Africa's Anglican Church.

Desmond Tutu, one of the most important people in the country, loved, respected and admired throughout the world, had now taken on the most important job ever held by a black person in South Africa. He talked on equal terms with prime ministers, monarchs and presidents.

Yet, because of the colour of his skin, he was still not even allowed to vote.

Desmond's enthronement, as the ceremony to become an archbishop is called, was an inspiring event. It was even more distinctive than the Nobel Ceremony two years earlier. There was joyous singing, dancing and prayer. Desmond invited politicians like Senator Edward Kennedy of the USA, sports and pop stars like Lionel Ritchie, Stevie Wonder and the tennis player Arthur Ashe as well as Coretta Scott King, the widow of the great American civil rights leader, Martin Luther King, with whom Desmond has often been compared.

Blacks and Whites mingled in the congregation in Cape Town's great St George's Cathedral: "How I pray that our Lord would open our eyes so that we would see the real true identity of each one of us, that is not a so-called 'Coloured', or White or Black or Indian, but a brother, a sister – and treat each other as such," said Desmond in a voice ringing with emotion and hope.

But the enthronement was a spark of light in a land that was becoming increasingly gloomy.

"Many observers believe that this irrepressible imp of a man who describes himself as a teddy bear, is the only figure holding back a tide of black violence against the state. One day white South Africa will realise, he believes, that he and other churchmen, thrust to the fore by the imprisonment or exile of black political leaders, have stood between South Africa and catastrophe."
Peter Godwin,
from "The Sunday Times"

"Tutu's influence is still considerable, but as the level of black anger rises, these appeals for restraint and Tutu's attempts to open a dialogue with the Government are slowly eroding it. Somewhere there is a point beyond which he may cease to have meaningful influence over the activists. If he passes that point, there is no national figure outside the jail cells who could replace him."
Allister Sparks,
from "The Observer"

Archbishop first

Now Archbishop Tutu's religious disciplines became even more important to him. He felt that the long hours he spent at prayer somehow "recharged my batteries".

"If I do not spend a reasonable amount of time in meditation early in the morning, then I feel a physical discomfort," he once explained. "It is worse than having forgotten to brush my teeth!"

He always started several hours of prayer at four in the morning. Then jogged for half an hour. But soon after becoming Archbishop, his ankle gave so much trouble that he had to take a brisk walk each morning instead. Breakfast, as usual, was a simple glass of fruit juice.

The days were spent receiving foreign visitors, giving press interviews and mostly giving advice and counsel to his bishops and priests. As Archbishop he felt this to be his main responsibility.

Several breaks for prayers plus lunch and a short afternoon sleep filled his day.

His highly-disciplined routine was a habit of over twenty years as a priest. He saw it as central to his life.

For relaxation he enjoyed listening to serious music and reading – mainly religious or political books. Time spent with Leah became increasingly precious.

Whereas before the newspaper headlines had concentrated only on Tutu's punchy political statements, they now focussed on his life as Archbishop. The deeply religious side of Tutu came as a surprise.

Many South Africans had condemned the appointment, seeing it as political. Very few knew of Tutu's academic brilliance or his deeply spiritual commitment. Fellow bishops knew that Tutu would have been a prime candidate for Archbishop if he'd never even made a political speech in his life.

But Desmond Tutu's political leadership was now going to prove absolutely crucial in the terrible days that followed. New laws which banned all remaining anti-apartheid groups now came into force, leaving the Churches as the only real opposition. Desmond Tutu's voice and leadership were now vital.

"... There is nothing the government can do to me that will stop me from being involved in what I believe is what God wants me to do. I do not do it because I like doing it ... I cannot help it when I see injustice. I cannot keep quiet. I will not keep quiet, for, as Jeremiah says, when I try to keep quiet, God's word burns like a fire in my breast. But what is it that they can ultimately do? The most awful thing that they can do is to kill me, and death is not the worst thing that can happen to a Christian."

Desmond Tutu, from his testimony to the Eloff Commission of Enquiry into the affairs of the South African Council of Churches.

The darkest days

The government, which had lifted the state of emergency, re-imposed it in an even more drastic form than before. The police and army were given almost unlimited power to imprison, torture and kill at will. Television cameras were banned from all troublespots. The press was savagely censored.

But among extreme, racist Afrikaners, an even more sinister force was coming to the fore.

It was a hate-filled, neo-Nazi political party called the AWB. Its members paraded with swastika-like flags, demanded a return to the hard-line apartheid of Dr. Verwoerd and actually condemned P.W. Botha for being too liberal!

It was to appease these frightening fanatics that President Botha banned peaceful opposition groups in 1988.

"We shall be free!"

Yet after so many decades of injustice, and despite all the continuing cruelty and bloodshed, the pressure on white South Africans to give up their supremacy grows irresistibly. It is no longer a question of whether apartheid will be dismantled. The only real question now is, "How long will it take?"

It could be many years. Many experts predict that the powerful state and its army can hold out for decades. Others fear there may be terrible bloodshed before apartheid dies. The crackdown of 1988 made an end to injustice seem as far away as ever.

But history is full of tyrannies which have crumbled and fallen. Archbishop Desmond Tutu – and the millions of other South Africans of all colours who share his dream – are certain the nightmare *must* finally come to an end.

As he has put it: "Many more will be detained. Many more will be banned. Many more will be deported and killed. Yes, it will be costly. But we shall be free! Nothing will stop us becoming free – no police bullets, dogs, tear gas, prison, death. No, nothing will stop us. God is on our side."

Even the mild changes to apartheid that have been allowed by the government have produced an extreme right-wing backlash.
Top: Neo-Nazi AWB leader Terre Blanche.
Bottom: However much these children and their parents resist change, change is coming.

Left: Prosperous workers in the streets of modern South Africa. Many Blacks are now moving into managerial jobs. Industry desperately needs their skills. To them, apartheid is already a nonsense. But will the police state allow the changes that have to happen? Will people like Tutu be able to make that change bloodless?

Below: Marriage between black and white is once again allowed. Desmond Tutu stresses that the people of different races get on well together. But, can this goodwill be sustained in the turbulent move to real freedom?

Important Dates

1931   Oct 7: Desmond Mpilo Tutu is born in Klerksdorp, seventy miles west of Johannesburg.

1943   The Tutu family moves to Munsieville in Krugersdorp.

1945   Tutu has tuberculosis and is in hospital for twenty months. He becomes great friends with Father Trevor Huddleston.

1950   Tutu leaves school with distinction.

1951   Tutu goes to the Bantu Normal College to train as a teacher.

1954   Tutu gains his teacher's diploma.

1955   Tutu gains a Bachelor of Arts degree from the University of South Africa. July 2: Desmond Tutu marries Leah Nomalizo Shenxane.

1958   Following the implementation of the Bantu Education Act in 1955, Tutu gives up teaching and starts religious training at St. Peter's College, Rosettenville.

1960   Tutu gains his Licentiate of Theology and is ordained a deacon in the Anglican Church. He goes to work in Benoni.

1961   Tutu is ordained a priest.

1962   Sept: Tutu goes to London to study theology at King's College.

1965   Tutu gains Bachelor of Divinity degree.

1966   Tutu gains Master of Theology degree.

1967   Tutu returns to South Africa to teach at St. Peter's College, Alice in the Eastern Cape.

1970   Tutu becomes a lecturer at the University at Roma in Lesotho.

1972   Tutu becomes Associate Director of the Theological Education Fund, based in Britain.

1975   Tutu becomes Dean of Johannesburg.

1976   July: Tutu is consecrated Bishop of Lesotho.

1977   Tutu delivers oration at funeral of Steve Biko.

1978   Tutu becomes General Secretary of the South African Council of Churches (SACC).

1979   Tutu first supports economic sanctions against South Africa on Danish television. He receives an Honorary Degree from Harvard University in the U.S.A.

1981   The Eloff Commission is appointed to investigate the South African Council of Churches (SACC). Tutu gives evidence in September 1982.

1984   Dec: Tutu receives the Nobel Peace Prize.

1985   Feb 3: Tutu is enthroned as Bishop of Johannesburg.

1986   Sept: Tutu is enthroned as the Archbishop of Cape Town, head of the Anglican Church in South Africa, Lesotho, Mozambique, Namibia, Swaziland, St. Helena and Tristan da Cunha.

Important Dates: History of Apartheid

1652   The first permanent white settlement is founded at Cape Town by the Dutch East India Company.

1820   The first British settlers arrive.

1835-54 The Great Trek: more than ten thousand Afrikaners leave the Cape Colony and trek north.

1879   The Zulu Wars begin.

1899-   The Boer War breaks out and is won by the British. Thousands of Boers
1902   die in British concentration camps.

1910   The Union of South Africa is formed. Black people are not included in the negotiations.

1912   The African National Congress (ANC) is founded. It is based on Gandhi's non-violent principles.

1913   The Native Land Act is passed: 7.3% of land is reserved for black people.

1927   A law prohibiting sexual relations between Blacks and Whites is passed.

1936   The Blacks' voting rights are abolished.

1948   The National Party wins the general election and introduces its policy of *apartheid.*

1950   Hendrik Verwoerd is made Minister for Native Affairs and encourages tribalism by promoting the authority of local chiefs.
The Group Areas Act and the Population Registration Act are passed – the two basic laws for separating the country's peoples.

1952   The Defiance Campaign causes a rise in membership of the ANC from seven thousand to one hundred thousand.

1955   The Bantu Education Act is implemented.

1959   Verwoerd passes the act which sets up eight national "homelands". The universities are segregated.

1960   March 21: The Sharpeville Massacre.

1961   Verwoerd declares South Africa a republic and withdraws from the British Commonwealth.

1962   Nelson Mandela is arrested and sentenced to five years' imprisonment. He is found guilty of further charges at the Rivonia Trial and in 1964 is sentenced to life imprisonment.

1963   The government introduces ninety-day detention without trial. Protesters are imprisoned in solitary confinement. In 1965, 180-day detention without trial is introduced.

1969   The Black Consciousness Movement is founded by Steve Biko.

1975   The Minister of Bantu Education instructs that arithmetic and social studies must be taught in Afrikaans in black schools. In June 1976, a peaceful demonstration against this ruling by fifteen thousand black schoolchildren in Soweto is fired on by police. Within days rioting spreads to several other townships. The unrest continues throughout the following twelve months.

1977	Sept 12: Steve Biko dies while in police custody.
1978	P.W. Botha becomes Prime Minister.
1983	Botha announces plans for a new constitution to include representation in one parliament for Whites, Indians and "Coloureds" in proportions that allow the Whites to retain control. The Blacks still have no representation.
1984	Violence erupts and continues throughout 1985 and into 1986.
1986	June: Botha imposes a State of Emergency. The Immorality Act and other petty apartheid measures are repealed.
1988	Feb 29: After three years of severe repression, Botha bans all remaining anti-apartheid organizations. The leaders of South Africa's main religions protest in Cape Town. Tutu and others are arrested briefly. During 1988, the police become more aggressive and are given more powers. The neo-Nazi right-wing groups gain support.

Glossary

African National Congress (ANC): Founded in 1912 to campaign for national unity and Black rights. The ANC followed a *non-violence* policy up to March 1960 when it was banned by the government.

Afrikaans: A language that has developed from Dutch. It is spoken by descendants of the *Boers*.

Afrikaner Weerstandsbeweging (AWB): An extreme right-wing party which opposes democratic rule by parliament and any form of concessions to "non-whites". It has a strong Nazi influence.

Anglican: Of, or belonging to, the Church of England or any church associated with it. A world-wide group of Christian churches which, unlike many other Protestant churches, have *bishops*.

Apartheid: Literally "apartness", it involves separate development or racial segregation, and became government policy after the 1948 election.

Archbishop: The highest rank of *bishop*. As Archbishop of Cape Town, Tutu leads all of southern Africa (including Lesotho, Mozambique, Swaziland and Namibia).

Bantu: The official South African government name for any *Black African*. Hence Bantustan – a *"homeland"* for Blacks.

Bishop: A priest who has the power to appoint other priests.

Black: The preferred description for all brown people. In recent years many South African Asians and *"Coloureds"* have called themselves Black as they want to show solidarity between all oppressed groups.

Black Consciousness: A peaceful opposition movement, founded in 1969 by Black university students. Its best known leader was Steve Biko. It aimed to reverse the morale-sapping effects of *apartheid* by encouraging pride in being *Black*.

Boer: Literally a "farmer" and a descendant of Dutch or French Protestant settlers in South Africa.

Censorship: The practice of preventing the spreading of information via the mail, the media (including books and the press), because it is considered dangerous or politically unacceptable. As a result of censorship, there is no news in South Africa of protest or violence. Many South African *Whites* are unaware of the reality of life in the *townships*.

Clearances: In 1948, the different racial groups sometimes lived side-by-side. In the clearances, the government moved 3.5 million "non-whites" out of white areas.

Colour: The crude attempt to classify people by their skin colour and other *"race"* characteristics.

"Coloured": An intermediate racial grouping between *Black* and *White* in official language.

Comrades: Young Black activists who took control in the *townships* during the prolonged period of unrest in the mid 1980s.

Dean: The administrator of an *Anglican* cathedral and head of a group of priests.

Detention: A legal way of removing people from public life in South Africa. Peaceful protesters can be held for 180 days without trial.

Eloff Commission: Set up in 1981 by Prime Minister Botha to investigate the *SACC*.

Group Areas Act: The basic legislation, passed in 1950, that defines where people can live and work according to their *colour*.

"Homelands": Another name for the Bantustans (see map on page 27). They form less than 14% of South Africa, but the vast majority of the black population (nearly twenty-four million) must live there.

Kaffir: An insulting name for *Black* Africans.

Native: Outdated official term for *Black* South Africans. Literally "native" means "born in the country". So, all South Africans are native South Africans.

"Necklace": A method of murdering suspected *Black* informers by placing a petrol-soaked tyre round the neck of the victim and setting it on fire.

Nobel Prizes: Instituted in 1901 in memory of Alfred Nobel. They are awarded annually for the world's highest achievements in medicine, chemistry, physics, literature, economics and peace.

Non-violence: A method of peaceful protest pioneered by Gandhi in South Africa. It requires people to break laws they feel are unjust but not to resist arrest or to retaliate, should they be attacked by the authorities.

Pan-African Congress (PAC): A more militant movement, started by a breakaway group of ANC members. The group was banned in March 1960.

Pass Laws: The first law was passed in 1809. It required all Africans to carry a pass when they were off their "master's" property. Greatly extended and strengthened between 1870 and 1980 to ensure the *Blacks* lived in the most convenient place for the *Whites*. Every Black aged sixteen or over had to carry a Pass Book and if caught without it would be fined or sent to prison. Recently these hated laws have been replaced.

Prejudice: Literally "pre-judging" or forming unfavourable judgements based on inadequate facts.

Race: A group sharing a common history, language, ancestry or geographical area. The concept enables some groups to presume that they are "racially superior" and can therefore treat other groups as "inferior". Genetic evidence now proves that only minor characteristics like hair type and colouring have a biological basis. Differences in specific talents, personality and intelligence within any one population group are enormous compared with differences between groups.

Racism: The belief that some *races* are biologically superior. This allows people to treat other races badly. Racism is not always *Blacks* being oppressed. Many people regard *all* "White South Africans" as tyrannical, although many thousands of white people have been jailed or exiled for helping black people. Lumping any group under one heading is racism.

Sanctions: Financial and military measures, used by one state against another, to encourage it to change.

South African Council of Churches (SACC): A grouping of many Christian churches to promote Christianity.

Tuberculosis: An infectious disease which most often attacks the lungs. Symptoms include coughing, spitting blood and loss of weight. It can be fatal.

Umkhonto we Sizwe: The name means "Spear of the Nation". It was the militant wing of the ANC and was led by Nelson Mandela until his imprisonment in 1962.

United Democratic Front (UDF): Founded in 1983 as an umbrella for hundreds of anti-*Apartheid* groups. Its aim was a non-racial South Africa achieved by *non-violence*. Its activities were severely restricted in February 1988.

Voortrekker: A member of the "Great Trek", which left the Cape Colony in an attempt to escape from British rule.

White: Any pale browny, pinky ex-European resident in South Africa. Whites form about 18% of the population.

Index

Further Reading

Addison, John: *Apartheid* (B.T. Batsford, London, 1987)
Benson, Mary: *Nelson Mandela* (Hamish Hamilton, London, 1986)
Birch, Beverley: *A Question of Race* (MacDonald Educational, Great Britain, 1985)
Cameron, F. & Kristensen, P.S.: *We live in South Africa* (Wayland, Great Britain, 1985)
du Boulay, Shirley: *Tutu: voice of the voiceless* (Hodder & Stoughton, London, 1988) [an adult biography, but easy to read and comprehensive]
Fairfield, Sheila: *People and Nations of Africa* (Young Library, Great Britain, 1987)
Gibbs, Richard: *Living in Johannesburg* (Wayland, Great Britain, 1981)
Huddleston, Trevor: *Naught for Your Comfort* (Collins, London, 1987)
Paton, Alan: *Cry the Beloved Country* (Penguin, London, 1970)